The Conditions

We Live

E.A. Johnson

The Conditions

We Live

E.A. Johnson

THE CONDITIONS WE LIVE
Copyright©2019 E.A. Johnson
All Rights Reserved
Published by Unsolicited Press
Printed in the United States of America.
First Edition 2019.

All rights reserved. Printed in the United States of America. No part of this book may be used or reproduced in any manner whatsoever without written permission except in the case of brief quotations embodied in critical articles or reviews.

Attention schools and businesses: for discounted copies on large orders, please contact the publisher directly.

For information contact:
Unsolicited Press
Portland, Oregon
www.unsolicitedpress.com
orders@unsolicitedpress.com
619-354-8005

Cover Design: Kathryn Gerhardt
Editor: Saidah Wilson
Editor: S.R. Stewart

ISBN: 978-1-950730-01-8

Acknowledgements

*Sing in me, Muse, and through me tell the story
of that man skilled in all ways of contending,
the wanderer, harried for years on end,
after he plundered the stronghold
on the proud height*

—Homer, *The Odyssey*

*I am a part of all that I have met;
Yet all experience is an arch wherethrough
Gleams that untravelled world, whose margin fades
For ever and for ever when I move.*

—Tennyson, *Ulysses*

I have thought often of the places in life and the people who made them great, and it is to people and places I owe much of this work. To all my friends who've put up with the incessant rough readings and bounced ideas like toys of the mind: my gratitude is never ending. To my family, especially my parents, Bob and Lee, who've supported me as I ran the gauntlet of school and work and art, watching to make sure that when I fall, I have the strength to get back up: much of my success is owed to you. Finally, to Amanda, the woman with whom I share my life and my love: I see in your struggles a picture of mine and in your success a celebration of determined hope. Words, even a poet's, have no strength to capture what you have done for me.

I give this work to you all, and leave it as Tennyson did *Ulysses*, "to strive, to seek, to find, and not to yield."

Table of Contents

The First Steps
A Resting Place — 2
Westbound — 3
Written on the Back of a Placemat from Crabby Bill's — 4
Epiphany — 5
Abbreviated Memories — 7
A Dirty Windshield — 9
Galway Nights — 11
edges — 13
Air Travel — 14
The Toreador — 15
Evolution — 17
Insomnia — 18
To Another, Killed in the Line of Duty — 21
Natural Derivative — 24

Chasing the Hobgoblins
Tasting Iron — 28
The Sculptor — 33
Precent — 34
The Poet's Mindcity — 36
Dreamer Sleeps — 38
Knowing — 39
Transcension — 40
on Words — 42

Funeral Stones	43
Letters to Lisa	44
Terrified	45
Silk	46
Tetrominoes	47
Scarecrows	50
These Houses Stand Empty	52
The Prophet	56
Worship	57
Quarrel	60
Shadows in the Cave	62
Tear the Page	63
Autumn Thought	65
Thoughts in a Coffee Shop	67
The Vagabond Sings of His Nightingale	68
Forgiveness	71
Ante up	72
Six-Year-Old Tomorrows	75
Flying	77

The Journey Home

we dance	80
Ant'anima	81
Cityscapes	83
Parts	100
This is Us Tomorrow	85
Imperfect Angel	87
Metamorphosis	89
Olympus Revisited	90

Causing Shadows	91
Artifice	93
Antihero	95
A Good Day	97
Irrelevant	98
You are My Paraphrase	100

The First Steps

"A journey of a thousand miles begins with a single step."
– Lao Tzu

A Resting Place

There used to be a bright garden down the street,
verdant grasses and tropical flowers.
It was my oasis in the concrete desert.
I would sit at the base of a peach tree
and watch the indigenous creatures wander back and forth.
When the sun broke through the clouds, the water would glisten softly,
but when there was no sun and the clouds moved in,
the garden never took on the sinister nature of the city.
Instead, it glowed with an inner light subdued by the city air.
The comfort I found at the base of that tree
provided a needed break in my modern day; my escape to nature.

There used to be a bright garden down the street;
it was my oasis in a concrete desert,
but now someone has painted over it, large bubble letters
spelling out *Justine* in neon blue and orange,
and on the water, an indecipherable symbol.
What's left of the garden is peeling slowly away from its brick façade,
exposing the city for what it is as the passing sirens swallow my oasis.

Westbound

Listening to canned music and skateboard chords,
I wait for the westbound train, alternating subway winds
blowing in my face, a buzz lingering in the early evening.
An empty track, and the quiet conversation of strangers.

Subterranean rails roar relentlessly in the singular night,
the squeal of a discontent fight for friction against inertia
scratches the rhythm of the platform like a stylus over vinyl
and I cross over, leaving behind only canned music and buzzing lights.

We are wanderers sharing a car, each in their private thoughts
ignorant of the fact that we are mere cameos in each other's lives.
Only the mother and her child, holding each other,
don't know they're alone as night plays silently.

Train doors that refuse to stay closed keep them,
the specters of the midnight rail standing still.
A man down the car rambles on about a door he once knew,
the words dying in the air before he can grasp their meaning.

Reflections of the exterior world against the subway window,
the lights and people mere reflections, shadows of the real,
like my words that disappear in the dark platform air
walking through the broken door into the imagined real.

The real only exists in darkness; the rest is shadow and light
below the other's surfaces, hidden in the shadows of the moon.
We fake the sun to find the comfort of facsimile
and derive meaning where none can exist.

Written on the Back of a Placemat from Crabby Bill's

Standing on the crowded shore
surrounded by people
all with a reason for being there
a purpose,

all save one.

The crashing waves encourage me to forget
while the sand invites me to engage,
and currents of the timeless waves
move like clockwork on the sands
and wash away any evidence.

I list across the water's edge
thinking of the future tomorrows
where this won't be a futile exercise
where the ever-expanding ocean will rise
and high tide will wash my vision
eclipsing the perfect horizon.

Lightning rips the sky in two
and tears me back into the world
falling down—gasping for breath
looking for a new resolve.

Epiphany

Corralled into oblivion, surrounded by the void
I undertake this problematic guise of living.
Now I stand here upon the seam of thought and hope.
Rational mind, irrational heart, warriors against the real.
What's right in one is impossible in the other, what is
And what can never be combines to form the walls of my cage,
Unreal, imagined, confining, shrinking and not withstanding truth.

How?

I live beneath the rock of my own conscience,
Consciousness withholding the inevitable oblivion of my creation.
Beyond the rock that was once stable, the roaring sea gropes
Reaching from my sanity, sanctity, sanctuary.
Transcension, dissension, descended beyond the shadows of thought,
Above the clouds and below the grave sit the unknown, destiny, deity.
Fate, fop, false, phony, fan of the fake pharaoh. The unreal, the
        unknown…
The undead.

To stand below the grave and know the truth, is it worth the effort?
Can one undermine one's persona, one's perceived notions of thought
Cognizance, innocence, obstinance, consonance, dissonance.
Dissolve the truth into the know, process, post-processed-past-
        possibilities.
Undermine the truth behind the things unknown to ourselves, but know
Somehow, somewhere, deep within, unutterably determined to hide our
        truth.

The self.

An idea born of the false prophet, lost in the false world of the false god.
The secured, procured, uncured, uncurable idea of broken bodies and
    souls
Littering the field of the unprotected mind, innocence is the cause and the
    cure,
The reason for and the way out. Unutterably, knowledge is power for
    destruction.

Abbreviated Memories

I feel the need to finish this,
piping hot and stale though it is,
this dram helps me skim the edges of life
and moves me back to the faith we had.
Our accomplishments have paled—
lost their meaning in the shadows.

We walk forward toward the center
of indelible arts. The paintbrush arcs,
painting the pictures still left in our minds.
All we've found is the stain of invisible ink
immutable against the backdrop of the nightly news,
as every voice cries out to be heard.

Finding our way in the ocean's sand
walking the beaches of a cultured mind.
We stand alone, lost in the crowd on the streets
of all the cities we call home.
We're waiting to find the feeling again,
youth has advantage, after all.

We used to fight against established creeds,
yell ourselves hoarse at the buildings.
The soul still young in a body getting old
coughing, wheezing, trying to catch
abbreviated memories, rushing past
with the speed of forgotten lust.

We watch the world with eyes refusing
to mature, to match the speed of time.
Clinging to our past, yearning for the fight,
I stand and call out to you
rushing past the pre-formed thoughts
of the times I knew myself.

A Dirty Windshield

Rain beats down on the river of concrete
pooling in iridescent puddles against the tar.
Through my dirty windshield, I watch the movement
as melting snow drowns the budding orchids
and the rotting leaves of last fall stop the drains.

Waiting for the deer to cross in front of me,
I'm reminded of the dog I watched last spring.
The truck hadn't stopped that day, and the dog,
end over end, at least a foot in the air, whimpering
in the road while I held the water, too late to save.

I'm shielded from that memory the bitter air would bring,
yet I can still feel the collapsing street beneath me.
I seek the insulation of modernity, the safety,
but I've lost the fellowship with the night
calling out to the frosty eye for filial grace.
My territory is marked by walls too solid.

Life is not found in the ditches of last summer's death
when we howled from the roofs of the earth,
the lonely trip back down when even the mosquitoes had left.
Life is not found behind a dirty windshield
in the insulation of broken roads.

Once, I knew my place, knew my foundation,
built my walls, strong and tall against the moon.
Clearstory lighting doesn't provide an escape,
and I didn't think to build a door.
Leaving was never part of the plan.
Now that I want to find a new place,

stake my claim on another pound of dust,
I don't know how to get outside.
Clawing at the walls hasn't helped me,
and all that remains are bleeding fingernails.

Galway Nights

With open arms the corner pub
calls the wander-weary traveler in,
a friendly chat
a pint of ale
while the downtrodden dance
a waltz of joyous souls.
In the corner minstrels sing
their fiddles and their flutes,
nothing in this light restrains
the rugged spirits free.

In the streets the lovers kiss
oblivious to passing crowds
of singing friends who chanced to meet
in this Galway night.

With tired eyes and lively souls
the pubs their doors do close,
an improv verse
a carefree laugh
their joy they pour into the streets.
The lilt of music in their hearts
leaning on each other's arms
going 'long the way.
Unfettered notes caress the breeze
of rugged spirits free.

The chance-met stranger
of this blissful isle
holds discourse in a brogue so sweet
in this Galway night.

The sun is set into the bay,
midnight's song be sung.
A quiet laugh
a seagull cries
the city rests its tired head
while revelers linger in the square,
airing out their spirits high.
Where every stranger's an unmet friend
the night to spirited silence set
the rugged spirits free.

So here's to friends we haven't met
and here's to sights so grand
for always everything is right
in this Galway night.

edges

on the fringes, the outside.
an outsider on the edge
of reality, his, yours, mine,
it's all the same.
tattered edges, sides that don't quite fit.
a corner piece in the puzzle,
something that should be easy, but
some things just don't work.
the edge of society, the corners
of life, alive unknowingly,
the center of the world,
your world, on the edges of mine.
i watch from the edge, knowing
not what i am watching
only what i see.
i don't see what you do.
i see dark, your ends at my center,
the edges of yours in the middle
of mine. the murky ends, your ends,
places you won't go.

— i live.

Air Travel

There is a tide in the affairs of men
Which, taken at the flood, leads on to fortune;
Omitted, all the voyage of their life
Is bound in shallows and in miseries.
—*Julius Caesar, IV.iii.218-221*

Today, the cloud tops look like cotton ball mountains,
like ocean waves rippled by a light breeze,
providing a place for the weather-weary traveler
staring out the window of technology's new fowl.
The curtain that divides us is drawn back
to show the inequity of mankind,
the plush first class hugs the rich who purchased their tickets
without concern for the bill that's left unpaid.
They, without the worries, travel in comfort,
while the rabble struggling to meet the ends
have to pay for their blankets and their luggage
because there is no heat at thirty thousand feet.

I wonder about the other travelers stacked atop each other;
do they notice the cotton mountains out the windows
or are there more pressing matters in their frames?

I have watched the clouds for years, every time I fly,
and I have seen many new worlds in them,
but I have not seen a way to get out
from the belly of Joana's sky whale.
Instead, I watch as we submerge into the ocean clouds
and drown in a reality we never asked for.
Watching the sky whale eviscerate itself
I can almost see Caesar's ghost
walk down the gangway and into the terminals.

The Toreador

The toreador stands his ground
firm against the onrushing bull.
Classical and elegant, a dance with disaster
form and precision against raw power.

Like a young toreador I stand aghast
against the words of a lover.
Fumbling with my cape, a dance toward disaster
youth and romance against all odds.

The bull charges, enraged by color,
charging toward the intruder, intent on injury.
He doesn't flinch, but he watches it come,
daring Fate to do her worst.

The words come, I see red.
The intruders to my love, happy to harm
I stand frozen, but I watch them come,
praying for Aphrodite to intervene.

The bull's horns catch the cape
red threads hang from the tattered flapping edge.
The toreador steps aside, a dance with the devil,
yet still he stands, ready for another round.

The words cut deep into me
goring my heart on their twisted horns, mortally wounded
this young toreador falls back, a dance with the devil.
There I falter and fall to the end.

The toreador bows,
and I am through.

Evolution

I remember when our problems used to be human sized,
before all the pieces of us began to fade
stretching themselves beyond their tensile strength without breaking,
while the rest atrophied through lack of forethought,
before the end of things became known through yesterday's clippings,
and the new beginnings were only news in the postscript of an essay.
Society was sacred, beliefs held close, a newborn baby's swaddlings;
life assured in the lonely losses of later years.
Now, there are worn jackets with solid soiled exteriors
holding against the winds of winter's thaw while we have worn away the
        lining.
The course outer shell chafes the baby skin below, hurting, protecting,
keeping the feelings raw while insulating the body in itself
devoid of any semblance of meaning, we itch and scratch,
the raw skin protecting us becomes red and irritating,
and we are no longer willing to wear the outmoded flesh.
Our own skin, as an outsider, argues while we tear it away,
and when it's gone, we are left huddled together,
a massless ecstasy of formless creation undulating,
unfit for our own natural covering but holding unwavering loyalty
to the vestiges we willingly discarded long before we knew the
        consequences.
Regretting our actions, we reach again for the coat,
pulling it over our inflamed limbs trying to make it fit once more,
but the torn lining sticks like our discarded skin,
and we scream in pain to a god who long ago forgot we were here,
leaving us on the shores of an atrophying world
to claw at the sand with our fleshless fingers,
silicone and salt stinging the senses that should not be,
while we, once human, crawl again into the sea and drown.

Insomnia

On nights when I cannot sleep
I'll sit in my living room and watch
the lights dance on my walls
street lights, passing cars
but the street lights don't dance
and the passing cars are rare
so I sit alone in my room
as the clock slowly ticks away my time.

Outside my window is a house
standard for the neighborhood
a box, like the neighbors, like me
the lawn shows a caring hand
landscaped by the family
solar lights lining the planting bed
so the flowers show up at night
for the passing cars to see
always for someone else
but the leaves haven't been cleaned
and there is a sticker on their door

The modern plague
the trash barrel, standing in the drive
has the bright yellow warning

A child ran across the lawn the other day
a little girl, losing her left flip-flop
she was getting her ball from the backyard
probably lost it over the fence
looking at the door, she didn't understand the mark
the foreign symbol to her was nothing

she was looking to see if she'd get yelled at
for going into the backyard
a quick glance at the windows, shades drawn
the furtive dash into the backyard and,
her mission accomplished, she ran back
down the block and lost her flip-flop again

The modern plague
the new symbols for a new age
a thin line on the door explains

Before that there was this couple with a little boy
that was before the snow melted
before the sticker on the door
they would come once a week
the little boy was Latino, wearing a large coat
he liked to play in the snow
throwing snowballs at the man before
they all went into the house, coming out again
hands empty, dancing to the car and driving away
their lights, dancing on my wall
there was a sign then, in the yard
blue and white and swaying in the wind

The modern plague
a sign of the times we live in
the tattered remains of the dream

There is a guy who comes by now in his pickup
rust on the fenders, painted green
he unloads his mower and cuts the lawn
puts the green clippings in a barrel on the truck
he has been in the house a few times
removed the memories from the house
the forgotten relics, their importance lost
in the rush to escape the inevitable
he brought wood over, saws hummed for a bit
but that stopped a while ago and he hasn't been back
he didn't bother with the street side of the side walk

The modern plague
leaves caked on the road
the gutter overflows

This happened here once, to my house
or something like it
the hurried exodus, empty promises
relics left hidden in the eaves
the passing world proceeds
unaware of the abandonment
this could happen again
this, the modern plague

To Another, Killed in the Line of Duty

Neva Rogers, Minnesota, March 21, 2005

To all of you who stand
                    and hold
                              the line
who uphold the values that we seek,
you stand on the front lines before
                                            the lambs
                                            and
                                            the lions,
you stand against the continued barrage
not seeing your assailant but knowing them
                all
                        too
                                well.
You are the newest soldier
                          (of misfortune)
fighting a war
                    (that no one will recognize)
to go to work means facing the very foe
                                    (you're trying to save)
commanded by those who do not know
                    (do not care)
                                  about your situation,
sitting behind their desks—
                    (safely)
                            miles
                                    away.
You hold
          your accolades, your accomplishments
                                              before you

a shield
>	against the multi-pronged attacks.

You call for help but are
>	(*ignored*)
>	not heard,
so in the face of your final moments
you hold the honor
>	a badge afforded your position,
>	>	(*your service*)
but honor won't protect you
>	(*from a bullet*)
ripping
>	through that thinning veil into
>	>	**flesh.**

Your sacrifice goes unheeded,
barley mentioned in
>	the footnote
>	>	of a footnote.
It has become commonplace.

There will be no grand parade,
no mourning public,
no medal of honor
>	will grace your final resting place.

Yet I will hold a candle—
those to whom
>	(*you gave your life*)
took it freely,
shot down by one
>	you sought
>	>	(*to protect*).

Halfway across the country
                        (I sit beside you)
hold you a martyr
                (for the cause)
a fellow soldier
                (in this unknown war)
a soldier
            a martyr
                                            a colleague
                        a teacher.

Natural Derivative

The candle of day flickers against the walls of a sickly sky.
To the west, on a hill, a silhouette against the darker half,
the citadel of progress chokes out the lightening blue
as it coughs up its vicious vapors on the pleasing plain.

I stand in the middle of the intersection,
in the middle of the road,
in the middle of the city,
in the middle of the morning.

Silently, the sleeping city suffocating under sycophancy begins to stir,
the great beast chokes up another bout of breath before me,
the great carbuncles burst forth upon the cerulean walls,
and the hum of life begins to flow through the city's veins.

I watch the cars float around me,
the cars that carry the life,
the cars that exhale mini carbuncles,
the cars that drive the progress.

The candle's light grows brighter in the distance, no wind able to
    extinguish,
a single flame now hung unceremoniously on the walls above me.
Mankind's new forest, his new land, awaking to another new day,
the repeated magic of twilight's half brother losing power through
    repetition.

I watch the sun stroll to its place,
the sun walking the usual path,
the sun sitting on its favorite branch,
the sun sitting on its favorite balcony.

The morning's crisp air rushes past me, spurred by a truck carrying trees,
synthetic life pushing aside the currents of reality for its own benefit.
I watch as the world around me claws the throat of itself only trying to
        rebuild,
reconstructing that which it destroys through the ever-present desire to
        create.

Chasing the Hobgoblins

*"A foolish consistency is the hobgoblin of little minds[. . .]
He may as well concern himself with his shadow on the wall."*
                              –Ralph Waldo Emerson

Tasting Iron

Helen Dushner, January 18, 2008

It was snowing that morning I remember
    because there was a two-hour delay and I had just reset my alarm
The phone rang, and I let the machine get it
    her tremulous voice came over the speaker in the other room
                                                                                 8:00
        "Call me when you get this . . . it's . . . well, gimme a call."

I knew what it was; there was no need to call her back

        "You don't have to come. It might not be…could be a false
            alarm"
    When
    "Do what you think is best . . . I'll understand"
    Now

I made the phone calls:

    . . . can you
            . . . thanks
                    . . . yes, I need coverage.

The drive over was hard. Crystal flakes settling on my windshield
    *it was snowing that morning, I remember because there was a two-
        hour delay*
It was raining inside, too, but the wipers didn't take care of that
    did I turn on the radio or listen to the snow floating?
                                                                         8:30

I walked into her room and heard it,
    so that's what a death-rattle sounds like

I couldn't help it.

She would have been upset.　　　　She could have been a movie star,
Knowing how she looked now　　　never went out unless she was dolled up.
she was a fragile shell of herself—　There's this picture of her at the beach—
laying in her bed, eyes closed　　　standing next to her Andy,
it was like she wasn't even there.　　she could have been Marilyn Monroe.

I listened to the air rattle inside her
    I remember it sounded painful
She inhaled shallow, laborious, slow
    It was snowing that morning
held it for a minute as if savoring the moments
    could be a false alarm
then the soft gurgle of the air escaping her mouth

    "It doesn't hurt her . . . doesn't even notice it."
   I do
    "that patch is more for the family, dries it up."
                                                        10:00

We called the priest.
    "We could bring in a harpist?"
    We laugh . . . Can't you see that . . . see her . . .
      "What the hell is that thing?"
    We laugh again . . . got any jazz?
    That's more her speed . . . Yeah, and a highball

Man, did she love to dance.
  "I remember when she would sing . . . beautiful voice."
  *"I remember when she would take us out in the snow and spin the
    car out."*
    It was snowing that morning I remember
                                                        1:30

The snow had stopped when the priest came.
    He commented on the beautiful day.
    I remember it was snowing
    The sun shone brightly

    Let us pray . . . Our Father,
        I bit my lip
who art in heaven, Hallowed be Thy name.
        it wouldn't be right to cry
Thy kingdom come, thy will be done,
        I tasted iron
on earth as it is in heaven. Give us this day
        the snow
our daily bread, and forgive us our trespasses
        I can't say the words
as we forgive those who trespass against us.
        I bite harder.
Lead us not into temptation, but deliver us from evil.
        blood from my blood, flesh from my flesh
Thine is the kingdom, the power, and the glory forever
        she taught me this
    Amen.

He leaves us. He was sorry, but he had to hurry. He had appointments to keep.

They turned her on her side. She looked more comfortable.
        "Do you think she can hear?"
        Yes

The other tenants murmur in the hall, they know
    It was snowing that morning
They gather at the door as if it were a nightclub
    she was a partier . . . boy, did she party

But velvet ropes keep them out
    I still taste the iron

    I wiped the stuff from her face.
        She would not have liked it
            ...she was always so particular about her appearance
what else could I do? It was settled in her cheek, the patch wasn't working thick strings running down her face, it looked uncomfortable so I wiped it
    away.
    What else could I do . . . she wouldn't have liked it.

                                                            2:00

She opens her eyes for the first time that day.
    It was snowing that morning
I kiss her forehead and say I love you.

I tell my mother her eyes are open.
    she coos softly to her,
        "it's okay, your Andy's waiting."
She was always afraid of the dark.
    "we love you"
    Laughing over her bed, my aunt and I.
        I don't even know why.
        "we love you, it's okay, go to your Andy"
Laughter

    hey . . .
        Is she...
            What?
                How do we...
                      she is.

The little girl, *newly old*, crawls into bed with her mother
    ...she cries

                                                            2:30

we sit, witnesses to why we were there
mouths that cannot speak, minds that cannot think

> *It was snowing that morning I remember*

that painful numbness that is left,
silence falls on us in heavy flakes

4:00

The only sound was the ticking clock on the wall.

The Sculptor

A rhythm found in the absence of time;
conductor-less, the symphony of discordant sounds
join together in harmony to raise a frame from the dust.
Like sculptors' hands, excellent to the task,
they mold the uncarved block into a vision.
From barren dirt to a place teeming with life,
a hole dug, emptiness, replaced, reshaped, resized.
Dead trees transformed into something more.
From straight to angled, a frame, a skeleton with wood for bone.
On the skeleton, like gods, they put a skin,
veins to pump the vital fluids through; power
to the heart of the home. It comes from nothing,
from a lack of space, an idea, a skeleton, a form.
After the power leaves, the body's occupant
abandons the form for something better;
always moving upward, forward, never going back,
the skin will fall away, the skeleton revealed again.
The work of the sculptor remains, seen
as though something that should be hidden;
it comes again, revealed by time, through time,
a veil lifted to denude the true art of the form.
Then to the hole it will return, rotting,
collapsing skeleton fills the hole from whence it came.
From the dust of the earth it was raised,
and so, as everything must do, will it return in time.

Precent

There is a light in the world that shines for some,
an oculus of the soul.
An airy thing, even when the world around,
borne down by the burdens of an imperfect creator,
stumbles blindly into the ugly dark,
lost in an arrogant ignorance,
pretending to find heart when humanity,
the rare flower of a rarer thought,
languishes, unwatered in a forgotten garden.

And then there's you.

The trembling voice calling out of the dark
looking for a sliver of hope in a hopeless world.
Your voice reaches my ear, pulling me from the maelstrom
of my own disruptions to a purer form.
Unkneaded dough unable to rise,
your song lifts my life from benign neglect
and, like the purer half of an angelic soul,
Persephone returning,
you coax a summer from this winter's thaw.

And now there's us.

With you as my compass's center foot,
though I run and flit like a falling leaf
I am comforted by the pull of your voice. The angel's breath
forever binding me in the warmth of your presence
precent of the hope and dreams we've built
these past years, when despite the desperate chances
that have arrived in our way, we persevere
and build something greater than ourselves:
a chord accord of our mutual salvation.

The Poet's Mind

The devil is in the page, lurking, waiting for his prey,
like a scavenger seeking its next meal, carrion and rot.
A poet's heart pouring out its words, its feelings,
the stink that comes from too much pleasure aching,
each line fit for the scavenger, the vulture of verse.
Like the ill-fated phoenix at sea, searching in vain
for his fire, his rest from which to be reborn,
such is the poet to passion drawn, and from the vestige
of physical pleasure come the barren plains of contentment.
A poet, the lover of the ages, filled to the brim with passion,
can in one moment be consumed by his muse and left
as carrion on the road for the vultures of life to pick at.

Oh, the devil is in the page for sure, when in this life
that which is pure can be seen as a danger.
When in this life, we find happiness, it is to the poem
as the ocean to the phoenix, a drought for age and death.
Like his true home, his binding life and death, the torment,
tremulous fire, such must be the poet's soul, for in that
there is true form of life. Magic in the absence of mirth.
For such a life is our lot to live, a monk of the muse,
striding from fulfillment to desire. Only in such a time
can we weave our magic web of words, to catch the gossamer,
so only thus can we catch the maiden heart, maddening our cause,
for within us lies the true curse and blessing all in one.

The devil is in the page, and lucky so he may be,
for it is there that the writer's magic lies. Between
our words are naught but what they are, and tales seldom say
of one whose work has ever lived so close to where one plays,
and still to both attentions shown, where prosperity be gained.
Poets cast our lot in life, a rose among the thorns, beauty
granted for the view, but wary be young traveler bold:
to touch the soft luxurious petals comes to costly gates,
as beauty withers from the touch and thorns too bite hard to bear.

The devil is in the page, no doubt, and for you still to know,
but a touch is worth the risk, young traveler, as you'll find.
The poet lives on beauty's touch alone, for risk is but a tryst,
and life is known only on the page where touch will dull the mind.
So, what a risk is held to bear, a writer's wish and work collide;
words go limp as sour stems when beauty picked does fade,
but still we search for our flame, like a phoenix ocean-bound.
In this tactile life, to a poet's heart it seems,
the devil is in the page, indeed.

Dreamer Sleeps

As the sun kisses the feathered wings of morning
and Titania's fairies drop the early dew,
as morning spreads into all of God's creation
I so long to look at you.

Shrouded sleeping eyes closed to life's frustrations,
any sign of pain washed clean away,
a tear of light drips upon your satin skin
as the fairies dance "Good morning" to the day.

And I, like wakeful Oberon, lay wanting
your sweet release from Robin's spell
so when your dew-drop eyes betake the day
their angelic hue is my sweet tell.

For all the midnight revels on this fairy shore,
for all life's little mysteries shown true,
in this blissful moment, I would ask that time be stopped
so in this heartbeat, for eternity, I could stay with you.

Knowing

Knowing what could have been is the hardest part.
Knowing what we both always wanted,
        the family, children playing in the yard
knowing that their parents will always protect them,
knowing we love them, and they are part of something bigger than themselves.
        I wish we could live
knowing that something could happen to them and let them make their own mistakes,
knowing they will trip and fall, skin their knees and get back up
        or break their arm falling from that gnarled tree out back that
            used to grow apples
knowing that if they failed, we'd be there
knowing how to make it right, with a kiss
        to stop the world's pain.
Knowing what we want might not be enough this time, but
it's the not knowing that's killing us.

Transcension

Call it a feeling and cheapen the worth.
This anachronism of the soul,
called on as the outward show
of the inward mind.

This false ghost,
haunting the unstable dreams of self worth
called upon
        by the weak to excuse their wrongdoings.
        by the strong to excuse their true desires.

To say that the lost soul of the disembodied spirit
could fall to such disrepair is an affront to the heart:
        The body's rose.
Seat for this discordant desire
truly called on by the veil of self-guile
the want to be
        a part
        apart

What a difference a space makes:
In that space comes the true confusion of the heart,
an explosion of what we once thought to be true:
With a space it calls for unity
yet once together it desires to be torn apart.

Such is the confusion brought on by this rose
the center of the matter:
> Conflagration or Coronation.
Crowning achievement of the lost soul?
A generation not withstanding itself
to call on those who came before,
one stand wherein it must, to itself, remain true.

The rose of life,
> fed by its own death,
>> like a phoenix come back over the ocean,
stands at the brink of its own destruction and laughs.

Talking in circles—turning your pen on end
to trust in the refuse of your own mind.
The flotsam of creation is the past burden called forth when needed.
This saintly anachronism of the soul
called on by those who fail to see the connection
between what was and what will be: a future in need of a past.
Transfixed on the brink of self worth,
held by the song of heartfelt tears.
We stand, paragons of self-discovery, lost in the mire of the soul;
Feeling that which cannot be called a feeling,
finding the rose of thought and soul in one flesh.

on Words

Words, words, words
you hide in them
when the best lack all conviction
and the virtuous step down,
then all is pontification
and idleness renown.

Stand and shout,
there are those who do,
the brazen and the bold,
the rude trample all the way
our leaders, under pressure, fold
and good intentions never stay.

We listen to their promises.
We believe their lies.
They promise a tomorrow
to make King Midas proud.
Pivotal to our survival, with the very marrow
of our bones, they make our shroud.

Let stand those whose conviction is backed with virtue
without which we are left naked in the world.

Funeral Stones

In Memory of Ruth Johnson

We piled ourselves,
five stones, three-part in the box.
We stood and watched, nothing happened
in the box before us, holding the last of a generation.

Her silvered hair framing the face that was finally relaxed,
finally resting after so long and so much struggle.

I never saw her legs that day, never since the operation in fact,
but I knew that inside that box were two shoes for one foot
my mother was specific about that, for propriety's sake.
When my mother told me, her voice shook, unsteady confidence,
but she would have appreciated the gesture, for propriety's sake.

We stood apart, the family, three huddles of private grief.
My mother and father, my aunt, my wife and I, separately together.
My wife was behind me trying to comfort feelings that she didn't know:
my regret, my fear, my anger.
We hadn't always gotten along, but she was part of my foundation,
a foundation shaken now once more, pulling me closer to the base.

As I watch my father's tears, my mother behind him, comforting,
I know that I will be in his place one day, a stone
burying the last of a generation.

Letters to Lisa

I saw someone standing there the other day
and thought of you leaning in that doorway
on the day that you left me standing in the rain
watching you close the door for the last time.

If I had only kissed you that night
a sigh would have dripped from your lips
and fallen on your doorstep,
instead the puddle formed around my feet.

Then I saw someone; they reminded me of you.
Standing like you stood that day, the accusing look
as if I had done something wrong by not doing
and made the mistake of trying too hard not to try.

Time has a funny way of moving on despite itself.
Your first child is grown, at least driving now
like the rain the night I stood and watched the door swing
gracefully on its hinges, you already beginning to show.

Not that it matters now, anyway—
I left you there at the same time, I turned
and walked down your sidewalk, ignoring
the rain that pummeled my shoulders.

I used to wonder why I watched the door close,
why I didn't put my foot in the way and stop you
from shutting me out again. It was that easy for us,
but we both know the answer to the question we never asked.

Terrified

I've watched the light turn green countless times,
idling in the travel lane.
People honk their horns and pass me by:
some yell, some curse, some simply shake their head.
The light turns green again.

The road has held my tires
begging me to drive, to move on.
The gas is running out and the light turns yellow.
People gather around my car and watch,
they don't know they see nothing.

The yellow sun glares at me
from the center of my metal world,
and I hesitate still. Red, an angry eye
stares from heaven, and I know I cannot wait.
I go full throttle down a dead-end road.

Sometimes a choice, even the wrong choice,
is better than no choice at all.

Silk

The fabric of air, floating softly in the summer sky
tantalizing and delicate, as if to shred at the slightest breeze
elegance unfettered, emboldened by its makers,
fibers seemingly inconsequential to the touch.

From the start, the cloth of kings,
now we wear it, you and I,
we drape ourselves as if we had the right,
as if we were royalty, and we steep in its caress.

Time has tested its strength, its bonds,
from the worm it's made, a thread of endurance,
warm beyond its weave, soft beyond its touch,
the underestimated fabric of essence.

Caressing each other, we swim in its effluence
as our hands explore the soft, open fabric,
our woven fibers thread together like lovers with
the soft, seducing succulence caressing you.

Tetrominoes

"We are part of the video game generation,"
she said,
       "playing Tetris with our lives."

I sat waiting for an explanation that wouldn't come.
Her words had come out, vocal cords vibrating the air,
that was enough for her,
no explanation needed. I should know.

I sat watching a fly buzz
between the window and the screen,
the summer sun making it drowsy.
I knew it was almost over.

   "I know you don't believe me"
the words dripped sardonically from her tongue,
forming a puddle on the floor.
      "You never really could understand me.
      Too damn focused on your books
                 your dead words.
      I'm here.
           I'm alive.
      Live with the rest of us."

I've always been a part of that world,
antiquated as I might be.
We can't be the actors anymore,
   there are no more stages.
I've tried to live with the savages,
      but I have seen the people there and don't belong,
      and having hanged myself in their lighthouse,

I can't go back.

"We've moved
        three times already
and we're about to go again.
                Packing our lives
in cardboard boxes.
              Putting ourselves in the truck.
It's so much
      fun
              like Tetris."

Her quiddity
as she turns us into synecdoche.
Does she know what she's done
with my dead words
      floating face down?

Frantic in its search for freedom
the fly bounces from the glass and screen
      dropping to the bottom of the sill.
I open the window to free a kindred spirit,
      one seeking comfort of the familiar.

I imagine crawling to the edge,
              falling into the box
as she closes it,
           sealing my fate
with the cardboard flaps.

But that fancy,
           disingenuous
as it is,
      doesn't fit us

                    anymore.
I no longer fit
            with our precious things
                  packed neatly
        into boxes,
and the fly,
        though it struggled,
        lays quietly on the sill.

I stack the box
        with the rest of them
in the corner of the room,
and notice the screen is already full.

Scarecrows

"Tell me everything will be okay?"
      her voice,
           hoarse,
broke the silence that sat between us
like a vulture waiting to pick the carcass clean.

"It will, I promise,"
        I said caressing her hair
    as she sat next to me,
           bolt upright,
           staring blankly,
                the pictures flashing across the television
    reflecting in our eyes.

Our silence weighted the room.
Made the air too heavy for the speakers,
too heavy for words.
Only the dog breathing at our feet.

            The private thoughts hung
            unspoken in the air
                    what was
            what could have been
    broken plans
                    what next?

The ordered chaos of the unspoken,
                    felt by both and neither.

Through the window
                        across the room
a light breeze dances
                        with the leaves
against the bright blue sky.

"I wish it was raining," I tell the walls.
    "*Why?*" her hand on my back, her music in my ear.
"Then nature wouldn't feel so indifferent."
    Her hand making small circles on my back in the stillness.
    "Maybe it's not indifference..."

    Still,
    answers remain unspoken
    unknowable
    in the silence.
    With the dog breathing at our feet,
    we huddle together
    like scarecrows
    in a storm.

These Houses Stand Empty

I.

These houses stand frozen in a sea of concrete,
in relief against the cold sky, sentinels to the city.
The rivers of yellow and black flash, always moving,
never going anywhere.
The snow falls unseen on the busy sidewalks
while the living ghosts pass by unseeing.
Pale lights in the windows of ice towers
burn coldly in the colorless sky where dreams have fled.
Empty eyes staring out at the snow.
New Babylon has risen from the ashes of greatness.
A crippled phoenix rising from its eternal nest
to search for a new view, a new vision on which to feed.

The empty forms grasp aimlessly for feeling.
Across town there is a matching city, part and parcel in every way
except here there's life.
The ivy climbs the towers, and the stone streets surge
their cobbled faces toward heaven.
Here they don't pretend. Here there's silence.
Marble monuments stand to hold their life,
forever telling of the beloved mother or father
who in life was little more than a nuisance,
now immortalized in stone. The stone is the mirror
of our own living monuments of a dead city.
Here the mourners gather, hollow forms of grief
to tell their stories to ears that had stopped caring while they could
and now lay deaf, though only six feet away.

All the while the snow falls unseen on the busy sidewalks
while the living ghosts pass by unseen.
Pale lights in the windows of ice towers
burn coldly in the colorless sky where dreams have fled.
Empty eyes staring out at the snow.
New Babylon has risen from the ashes of greatness
A crippled phoenix rising from its eternal nest
to search for a new view, a new vision on which to feed.

The empty forms grasp aimlessly for feeling.

II.

Decorations line the eaves with elegant delight
and Winter's flowers stand on the porch in spite of the cold.
Accompanying lighted walks, the trees aglow
with season's cheerful blight.
The half-drawn windows wreathed in light
from the electric candles, placed with care,
fiercely fighting the frosting edges
as Winter's spider weaves her web across.
The fresh snow blanketing the walk
lies untouched by shovel or foot
though carolers sing
their Sleigh Bells Silent Night Noels.

Placidly the house looks on.
Its pale, half-veiled lids dimly flickering
as if recognition existed.
In the front yard a Santa balloon,
deflated in the glaring light of day,
stands erect as the magic of twilight descends.
The white metallic frames of reindeer stand rusting in the sun
magically transform when the current awakens their sleeping forms.
Seeing no sign of life, the carolers move on
down the street to houses much the same.
A glowing manger, a snowman balloon,
the odd change here and there.

But always the half-drawn windows wreathed in light
from the electric candles, placed with care,
fiercely fighting the frosting edges
as Winter's spider weaves her web across.
The fresh snow blanketing the walk
lies untouched by shovel or foot,
and though carolers sing
their Sleigh Bells Silent Night Noels

placidly, the houses look on.

The Prophet

I used to imagine that I could part the clouds
like some insubstantial Moses,
then I'd bring down the rays of sun on anything I wanted:
the billboard for canned peaches,
the blade of grass which fascinated a child's mind,
or the little puppy, unaware of the centuries of men behind its breeding.
I would play those rays like the strings of a giant viola
and listen as the music cracked into untuned life.

I've stopped imagining that I could control the clouds.
Something like that comes with too much responsibility
and I don't need that anymore.
Those radiant beams fall from the burning gas just the same
but there is no direction, no guide, leastwise not me.
The city buildings have long ago cut my strings anyway.

I can martyr the natural in this world as they have done;
the magic, and all that comes with it, is not needed.
I'll sit and accept the inconsequential if it means I can exist.
Besides being an insubstantial Moses,
leading a phantom people to some long dead Eden
is too much effort nowadays.
The child mind that played the rays of sunlight
needs to grow up eventually.

Besides, who would want to do more than exist anyway?

Worship

"I'll suck your dick behind the altar"
    she says,
"don't look so prudish,
        no one cares anymore."

The cantankerous Christian cacophony roars below
    while above, the cellular steeple sends out its signal
    high above the bells that stopped ringing
    because the neighbors got an injunction.

"You mean you've never had sex in a church before?"
    she laughs,
        throwing back her hair,
            hoisting her supple bottom onto the altar,
    willing to sacrifice herself for me,
urging me to sacrifice myself for her.

A bird's wings flap above us,
    her laugh having roused it from its roost.
    Someone left the doors open last year and now it's trapped,
    feeding on communion wafers and holy water.
    It lands on the baptismal fount and takes a bath.

She takes my belt and pulls me in,
    engorging me against the altar.
Her soft, nurturing lips press against my neck.
        "I want to fuck you against the choir box"
she coos into my throat.

Perched in the rafters, the bird watches the empty pews,
awaiting the coagulate congregation.

A cry of ecstasy from the people below,
    in the basement the church fair roulette wheel landing on double
        zeroes.

"Make me see god" she said
    rubbing her hands against the inner thighs of her jeans
    opening herself to the world, the pews,
        "the most religious experience in this place"
sweet Jezebel puts her hand down my pants.

The feathered fiend chirps again
    wings carrying it onto the altar
    waiting wafer, *corpus christi*
    once again takes it high above.

Her pure white wrist disappeared, reappeared
    rhythmically into the waist band.
        "We used to care" Jezebel chirped.
She took the phone out of her pocket
        the rectangle disrupting her smooth lines, offered on the
            altar.

In the basement they cry again, the craps table ministering to their needs:
    they stand in small crowds by the stickman, watching the shooter,
    they stand alone talking into the air
    their finger on the plastic preacher in their ears.

She slid down from the altar
        her warm touch withdrawn
    "get up there" demanding, turning me around,
pushing the vestments of my resistance to the floor.
    I raised myself on the altar, awaiting my offering.

        Her hair was smooth and smelt of lilacs.

        Wings ruffle above,
                      frightened by the noise.

I move my left hand for balance
        looking up the cellular steeple, the entrails of sacrifice,
    a silver tray falls roughly to the floor
        scattering wafers on the burgundy rug
        wings, frantic, beating against the air
the wafer falls forgotten next to a discarded feather.

The voices from below murmur a prayer for greed,
the plastic rectangle on the altar vibrates unheeded.

The squawk from above, lamenting the lost *corpus*,
the cross above it all silently sacrifices itself to progress.

Quarrel

When on this windless acre stand I thus,
the lonely pilgrim of an ancient land,
interred in thought on this dusty pound of flesh
when the tempest tossed song of progress spurs me on.

I have legs that do not walk.

So stand I surrounded by the wind,
intangible and yet violent thing it is,
known for its unmitigated wrath,
its undoubtable power to lift.

I have a mind that does not think.

To be one grain of sand upon that wind,
lifted to the heights of the desert vulture,
soaring above this carrion feast,
this pound of dust to which I cling.

I have hands that do not feel.

The wind moves in, surrounding all sides
crying out with the most unintelligible
primal screams of rage. I yell back,
reasoning with this cloud of dust at the top of my lungs.

I have ears that do not hear.

I shake my fist and scream to be heard,
but the crowding blades of sand shut me out,
and the only sound is the din of their mindless derision
as I await their coming storm.

I have eyes that do not see.

I watch as grain by grain the sand around me lifts,
trusting its weight to the crowding winds. And I, but watching, feel
there is reason to be moved, yet how can I find quarrel
in a grain of sand when honor's at stake.

I have a heart that does not beat.

Looking up as the last circle of blue sky disappears,
I see the *trógán* sun for what it is.
Feeling the ground swell beneath my feet,
I rush the veil and quarrel with the sand.

Shadows in the Cave

The tresses of the mind hold strong,
gilded tresses hanging low over the veiled light;
beneath the veil, thought glows bright, illuminating
the dark recesses that, every day, inch forward.

It is within this light we're held,
sitting alone as if in front of a hearth
where shadows from the flames dance on the wall
and strong light fades while darkness stands guard.

There is a small window to look through,
the only one allowed in this prison of light.
It's high up, above the fire, within the darkness;
and shadows are moving past, shapes of the world.

The veil drowns out all sound and touch,
numb to all, but the fire shadows on the wall,
they are our friends, our only companions
beneath this veil, within the prison, they watch.

The veil moves in the wind fluttering, moth-like,
and a corner hits the flame: beginning to devour.
As the fire consumes the veil, the tresses are seen:
tarnished, cracked, and weak—they wait to fall.

Tear the Page

This place will not be my tomb.
Institution gray and beige walls
Intent on cutting off creation
building futures, overcoming pain
Stop—

Not overcome 'cause that implies a struggle.
Action on the part of those developing
But that's not what's happening, not now
Scraping, grinding, dulling the blade
Once meant to cut above and through
obstacles, ideas old, and status quo
No—

Now it's softening, a rounding of the corners,
Childproofing the future.
Estrange a generation from pain,
Infantilize, prioritize, marginalize,
Paralyze a generation without aim or focus,
No guessing, no messing with potential.
A generation living in a padded world
Training only to listen and do, never create.
Codify the coddled generation of mitigation and alleviate,
Just defy the modeled hesitation to creation and meditate—

Justify a new beginning, leagues away from winning
Confound confining layers of denial,
Of reasons why, excuses not to try.
Redouble, double down, don't wait,
Don't hesitate, let the world sedate.
Exonerate your mind, find time, tear through.
Carve out the blocks of beige, create, break, bruise—
Let the world come 'round to you.

Autumn Thought

A cloud floats across the autumn sky,
its supple form changes with the wind
as dancers on a sunlit stage;
the colored leaves twirl and spin.
The clock is stopped, time sits
on this tattered bridge, waiting.
As all nature sighs with completion,
every balance of the year is met:
each morning the sun would rise
and again each night would set.
But now as Mother Nature walks,
her tired head hung low, to bed;
as the world moves to winter's slumber,
I gladly wait upon this tattered bridge of thought.
And on the waters of the lazy stream below,
in nature's ever-flowing looking glass,
I see the one for whom I wait.

Like the warmth of spring in autumn's night,
her eyes, like fireflies, shine,
and to my heart her love,
like a butterfly, delicate and free,
comes fluttering with high delight.
Her hair, soft and fragrant, a wisp,
a breeze on a gentle summer night,
floats about her face, falling,
like gossamer, upon her shoulders.
Her lips, like tulip buds, spring's messenger
pushing through winter's last snow,
from which sweet honey words,
that which would make the very bees jealous

and the flowers green with envy,
I long and love to hear.

There is no winter's rest for me,
no autumn slumber as nature
in all her balances would seek,
for while my love abides by me
I will be in spring eternally.

Thoughts in a Coffee Shop

Sitting in our solitary caves of thought,
modern miracles from a godless generation
searching for the lost meaning in our
self-made prison of intelligentsia,
our voices crying out in unison against
the concrete jungle that passes for our home.
Abandoning society's lost battles
to the darkening depths of instant gratification,
our drug of choice, our IV of happiness,
dripping slowly from the needle of self doubt.
We talk, saying nothing, having felt nothing,
numbed by our secret drug of choice,
our absinthe, allowing us to absent from life,
sustaining our meaningless drivel from thoughtless tongues
that worship nothing, having lost all faith
in the grace of a god that society has killed
by the very devices we wish to escape.
We sit in our happy hell of life,
every molecule a tempest of energy,
fleeing from our sorrowful lot
into the unending libation of our elixir.

The Vagabond Sings of His Nightingale

*Go to, sir; you were beaten in Italy for picking
a kernel out of a pomegranate. You are a vagabond
and no true traveler.*
—*All's Well that Ends Well*, II.iii.275-277

Winter's cold cruel eviscerative power
    known to chill the bones of Gaia
Demeter's curse on the world for the loss of her daughter
    taken by a man she did not love

free,
    but for a small red seed,

        Persephone's arranged marriage
        her walk, her peaceful lot, torn in two
            a cruel cold that will last until her return.

Was there another way before you?
    Demeter's curse the constant state of being
knowing only the open meadow blanketed and hidden from view
    lost to its brightly colored denizens

alone,
    but for a small red seed,

        unknowing of another way
        between the cold and the ground, an ember
            smoldering in the vacant lot, the blanketed meadow.

Like the hidden rubies of a hard-shelled pomegranate,
        hidden from view of undiscerning eyes,
the ember glows ignorant of Demeter's curse
          ignorant of the winter it chose to confront

ignorant,
        but for a small red seed,

        of what was there that had not been,
        you saw something in the vacant cold
            revealed something in the thawing hoarfrost.

Since I have known you, since we were
        Persephone's return eternal,
The ever-present Spring winds brush the roses from your cheeks
        and place them in the vacant lot

but for a small red seed,
        this vagabond

        this wanderer of seasons finds the coverlets have grown warm
           with you by his side, my Persephone, my Juliet
              my nightingale.

I will sing my praises to your immortal Spring
        to the flowered fields surging with the winds
and thaw my most unworthy of eyes
        of their hard shell and reveal

but for a small red seed,

        I would be lost

having found my worthy nightingale, the sweet juices of paradise,
having found my Persephone and her garden
    we build on the newly thawed permafrost, the
once-vacant lot.

Forgiveness

in memory of Sayvon Robinson, December 9th, 2005

There is little I can say
                         to ease the troubled thoughts,
A mind encompassed in the way,
                         a time when thoughts are dark.

       Good Lord You say of it a sin
             To leave before You call,
                   Besiege You yet the innocent
                         Beset with troubled fall,

And still in pain and sadness sit
                             the many left behind;
They sit and ask if You'll forgive
                             who has Your love in mind?

       Your forgiveness for him we do ask
             Admission to Your loving gaze,
                   In goodness lived this troubled lad
                         And to Your love we ask him raised.

       A friend he was to all mankind,
       To mode of passing we pray You're blind.

                   Innocence in childish grace,
                   Let him stand before Your face.

Ante up

"I'm sorry," he repeated.

Her eyes were cold and distant,
                                    her hands absently shuffling the deck.

He set the glasses down and sat across from her,
        his back to the yard,
leaning against the rigid chair she fell in love with last summer at the store.

Her hands moved deftly, each card moving in and out of the deck,
    switching places with another,
                                the stock backs hiding their truth.

Her eyes mischievous in the twilight,
                              her lips drawn thinly across her teeth.

Her hand flitted like a moth across the table,
                the cards gliding toward him,
                            bouncing off the glass,
    their effortless motion thrown askew and halted.

Condensation gathered on the glasses,
                              sitting heedless between them.

"You should have paid attention" she said.

He tossed in the blinds,
        big and small,
    and pulled at the corner of his pocket,
                                      looking at his cards,

"I tried," his worn words slid easily
                from the ruts they'd dug in his tongue.

    "Still," she said tossing out the flop, "you should have paid attention."

          King of spades – Two of hearts – Queen of diamonds.

              She added her money to the pot and dropped the street.

                  King of diamonds.

"It's not that and you know it," he said tossing some coins into the pot.

    The sweat rings expanded under the glasses,
          islands of water spreading,
    threatening to flood the street.

      She matched his bet and reached for the river,

"You never raise," he said.

    "What?"

"You never raise," he repeated. "You don't add to the pot."

        She tossed in a couple of coins.
        "Happy?" her voice, soft as the winter's breeze.

           He knew her raise was short,
                      but he matched the blind.

      She tossed the river,
           the card slid into the rivulets from the glasses,
        he pushed it back from the water.

Eight of clubs.

He added his coins to the pot,
                setting down a neat stack of five.
    She tossed hers,
            knocking over his stack.

"I call," she flipped out her pocket.

                      Queen of clubs – Two of spades.

"Always playing it safe," he said tapping a finger on his cards. "I wish you'd raise the stakes once in a while."

        "At least I call," she said, raising her eyebrows. "It's more than you do."

He tugged at the corners of his pocket again,

                    Valentine's Day – The Royal Couple, suited.

    He pushed his cards forward,
                stock side blankly up.

"I fold."

Six-Year-Old Tomorrows

I am a man alone,
lost in the transitions of
yesterdays
        and
              tomorrows
where today is the boot
under which my destiny is
(un)made.

We often find ourselves here,
at these places, without really knowing.
We overlook them because we are too
    tired
    hungry
    poor
    sad
    defeated
    weak
because we are too much of life,
but not the one we dreamed of
at six, under the shade tree,
eating stolen strawberries behind Pete's house,
licking the juices running down our fingers.

We're too much of the life we made
        of bills
        of responsibility
        of Sisyphean struggles,
and at that moment we realize
Camus had it right all along.[1]

As we repeat the process again
for the fifth time,
we see in the residue
the us we are.

The us of yesterday's past mistakes
living for the six-year-old's future
before living got in the way of life.

And so the six-year-old us
drops the stems of those sweet strawberries
(sweeter still for having been stolen)
under the tree and returns to exploring
previously mapped out woods of our neighborhood,
the day's dirt spoiling the sweet juices on our fingers
while a lucky ant finds our discarded stems
and (knowing his role to play)
brings a small piece back to his queen.

---

[1] Albert Camus' conclusion in "The Myth of Sisyphus" where he posits that "One must imagine Sisyphus happy."

Flying

He watches the falcon play along the crags
swooping through the pillars of stone
as the ocean breaks, wearing away the bedrock
foundations of the land.

All while the dirt clings tightly to his boots,
holding fast as he tries to pull away.
He bends down to grab the earth in his fingers one last time.
His shirt tightens across his back,
unwilling to open, the cloth like a shackle to his will.

    Feeling the cool, damp dirt.
    Feeling the solid base he's built his life on.
    Feeling the anchor weighing him down.

So he readies to leave what he knew,
from the safe and the secure,
to build a new foundation on the diaphanous clouds.

The tension coils in his legs,
ready to launch him from the places he once belonged,
outgrown as he is from his childhood,
and like a shirt too small for his new life,
his springs released from their confines,
his muscles tighten and push away the ground.

The short burst gives him almost no lift
as the cruel dirt pulls him down once more,
but he is unwilling to return to the confines of the dirt,
longing to wipe his boots on the cotton clouds.
The worn threads of his bindings give

with a scream both primal and cultivated,
he spreads his wings,
battering the lower breezes as he fights to rise.

>Rise above the cool, damp dirt.
>Rise above the solid base he's built his life on.
>Rise above the anchor weighing him down.

As the ground drops away like a wrinkled shirt,
>he rises.

As the draw of the dirt, sirens of the known, quiet,
>he rises.

As his old foundation drops away,
leaving nothing more than a cloud dimmed cliff,
>he rises.

He flaps his wings against the buffeting ocean winds,
the updraft driving him even higher
above the petty concerns of his past,
above the last remnants of his tired life.
The diaphanous curtain parts to the expanse
rising before him.
Soaring through the parting clouds,
the falcon floats weightless on the blasts
and with a powerful stroke the man overtakes,
he rises above and skirts the curtain of the sun.

The Journey Home

*Don't adventures ever have an end? I suppose not.
Someone else always has to carry on the story.
– J.R.R. Tolkien*

we dance

we dance
our bodies move in time with the music
the music—the pervasive beat flowing between us—around us
through us

it moves us
the music feeds our souls—feeding on us
through the beat it devours our inhibitions
it frees us

a look
one single look that would set the world on fire
teach the rock within to beat again—to feel
her eyes

a hunger
felt in her movements against me—toward me
emptying the crowded room until we are alone
together

i wonder
does she see my hunger—my want my need
for her—her heart and tender arms around me
we kiss

the world spins
we reach the peak—a pinnacle of the moment
the hunger is fed only to grow stronger within us
the song ends

Ant'anima

A race of giants had lived then, fearless men,
men of a staunchness unknown in this day.
                              —John Steinbeck, The Leader of the People

Where are the giants for whom the world was made?
They have been hobbled at the knees, cut down
by want, by ease of life, by the multitudinous crutches
afforded by modernity. Even the once-seen giants in ourselves
have lost their vigor with the push from our nests.

Atlas, the foundation of the world, lays broken
like a new Colossus at the bottom of the universe.
What is left of the world floats with amorphous support
tottering on temporal columns of space
while Atlas's shattered form slowly rotates in the Oort cloud.

We have erected the monkeys to stand guard for us,
so we never have to face our Oni. They walk around the outskirts
with our dragons and our demons, but none hold the gate.
We have given the charge to others to watch for us,
they in kind have turned it over and left the monkeys on the other side.

Where are the makers of mountains? Zipacna, who helped the weakened
        multitude
only to be betrayed, who survived by ingenuity. The makers of mountains,
the builders of the world made arrogant by their strength
and the weakness of others. Crushed by the mountains they built,
indurated by those who cannot do what they could.

Have we all been delivered so far from the jaws of Ægir
we have forgotten? He packed it up long ago, with his boiling pot
and ubiquitous libations, exiled to Saturn's frozen moon.
A sought-after host, a giant among men, disgusted
with our new desired weakness, swallows the sallow ale.

There are no more usurpers of heaven with unwavering wisdom and word,
they have all been devoured with the third step in Mahabali's bargain.
When the word was law, there were those who ruled with care,
whose generosity made the people happy. Where are they
who, despite the loss, retain their honor while the world succumbs?

We have lost the giants of this world, chained them to a rock and none remain
to set them free. Zeus's chains that bound Prometheus
were never as strong as the shackles born unto mankind,
whose roaring ocean is nothing more than a bourn dried by the summer
       sun
while we go hoarsely to wander in the desert that remains.

Cityscapes

It starts with rain falling down in sheets, droplets of glass
tumbling unchecked past the clouds, through the air,
hitting the trees and the grass on its incessant way to the ground.
The soil soaks itself in the bounty and the world becomes mud.
When the deluge lessens and the setting sun shines from the tops
of glass-barked trees, the colors spectacularly brilliant against
the still grey sky, the fire of greens and yellows and indigo.
The sun explodes on the horizon, sending shards of light
bouncing from the clouds, the glass-barked trees shatter,
the flowers, drooped under their newfound weight, wither,
as the grass tries to catch the shards of light in little beads
only to be struck down by their droplets of greedily gathered glass.

In the harsh light of morning,
empty houses with rotting roofs
stand next to overcrowded schools
with windows of brick and mortar
and churches with locked doors.

ÞURT

The precipice stands before the door, and I'm on the outside
stepping into the air, breath from an aphid's wings holds me up.
The gossamer webs of mendacity stretch within the depths.

Beneath that, poetic fountains flourish.

To hold that alexandrite of thought,
to drink from those life-giving fountains—
but it is not to be.

I'm kept aloft by the dust from a moth's wings
only to watch a butterfly hover just out of reach
and fall into the cold embrace of eight-legged mendacity.

A lamentable fate to be sure,
but I'm held in place by the knell of the steeples,
tarred black against the sun.

The rain falls,
easily slipping past mendacity's web
making ever-expanding ripples in Mimir's Well below.

It doesn't really matter, though,
because unlike the one-eyed god hanging from Yggdrasil,
I cannot get past the diaphanous web
to reach the stones beneath.

This is Us Tomorrow

I know it's temporary.
Everything is, after all—and it's not.

    We grasp the headboard to steady us in the fight,
pushing ourselves away from what we have—
    what we had in that special moment before the world stepped in
    and found that one little spot.

    A crack in our siding,
        just enough
            to let the water in,
        just enough
            to let it freeze,
                and in freezing,
expand beyond our limits and our plans.

    It's like those signs we see along the road
    we drive down daily to get to work,
    the one by the cliff:
    watch for falling rocks,
    the ones that early winter throws in our way,
        the grouchy old man messing up the smooth road we planned.

And our siding swells as winter tears at our door, clawing to get in.

    Like Papa said in his snarling voice, raspy around the edges,

The world breaks everyone
                and afterward
                many are strong
                at the broken places.[2]

---

[2] words from "Papa" are taken from Hemingway's <u>A Farewell to Arms</u>

Water has a way of pushing apart,
                        of carving a path through the hardest stones.

If nothing changes, it will place a canyon between us
        and we will be left lying here
                                      on opposite edges
                staring out into our own broken places.

Imperfect Angel

I stand naked and alone on a precipice of the heart,
before me hovers my Imperfect Angel
behind, the cold, hard valley of sterile stone.
A single rose grows beside me, turning its face
to the eye of God, the light of love.
Around this lonely flower, two butterflies play,
gracefully sliding in and out of the gossamer drops of morning dew.

My Angel hovers still.

Her hair, dark as night's veil, falls framing her face;
her eyes, deeper than the deepest ocean, look upon me softly,
softer than a petal that wilts when picked.
The curve of her face speaks confidence in volumes
and her lips, not as red as any rose, call to me.
They hold me in their notes, tenuous and still,
bid me come to her and, like the butterflies, we will play.

Oh Love, grant me wings that I might fly to her!

Cursed Sirens of Safety, call no more!

How easy it would be to turn and walk safe another day.
The uninviting valley talks of sense,
writhing in its own desolating, apathetic wind.
A man of sense would know where the Sirens live.
Their call comes from the hole
left when faith, to reason, submits its hold.

Still the Sirens sing to me.

Still my Imperfect Angel calls.

I stop my ears to the sensible song,
the safe alternative to living.
The Sirens song stops,
yet still my Angel calls.

I step toward her.

Metamorphosis

I see your willowed eyes in the darkness
on the window frame of night's cool embrace.
The broken musings of a poet's heart resurface
and from these nightmares I hide.

My silent words have found a voice again
in the stars of the half-broken window in the run-down house.
The shutters I thought were locked have come unhinged
while the frets of measureless music throw them open
and through this unrequited vow of silence,
the unsanctified monk withdrew from the cloister
of human decadence to the self-riotous field,
bathing himself in the river of self pity
flowing from the decimated spring from which Alfather drew the stones.
Mimir would be proud of this silent house I tried to build,
surrounded by the dying orchids of last spring.

I still remember when I could throw a lasso around a cloud
and pull it down to earth where I could feel it.
There was a certain power in that desperate youth,
the once-forgotten wonder of the wandering stars.
But the anvil on which my wit was forged
pounded out that magic, cooling my metal, shaping the will.
Now I wonder why the stars moved to that broken house
and where the clouds found room enough to sleep.

The dollhouse dreams of my abandoned mind
cry out in pity for the muted eyes and blind tongue,
asking why the stars are encased in glass
and why the trees were planted in such neat rows.

Olympus Revisited

You have been called by many names;
the world has drawn you many times
and draws you still from sea or star
as you emerge, a woman in full gait,
from the belly of the shell.

Your modesty in a coverlet of flowers
and your curious smile, captured
four centuries before your birth,
hang on a wall in a country you've never seen
named for a man who couldn't find enough apples for your beauty.

Yet in all of your depictions, be it paint or wood or stone—
Pygmalion himself could not capture you,
a beauty transcendent to the stars and stones,
enough to shame Galatea back to her pale slate—
they have denied you of your finer self.

You stand, apotheosis of a full-wrought beauty,
where each line traces an apogee of grace
and pride, well fought and earned, drapes like a chiffon dress
adorned not with gaudy useless bobbles
but girdled in a simple, gilded sash of pale green.

Neither sensual Venus in her open shell,
nor the mystery of Da Vinci's lady,
nor the seeming perfection of the Pygmalion princess
could draw from the praises of a thousand decades
what is felt for you by one man.

Causing Shadows

An echo of the unacted action,
hollow man filled with faces
clawing at the feet of the world,
becoming one's self through unbecoming
and words spoken without utterance.

The outmost face, the façade of all,
stands as the levies to the flood;
it will hold until needed most,
then crumble into Shelly's shifting sands,
covering the pedestal unworthy of words.

The next is the wanderer of the stage.
A split mask of laughter and tears,
white porcelain to hang on the wall,
watching for the humor, laughing at the tears,
mocked even by a curious chorus of angels.

The crumbling tertiary, taped together,
held close only by a thin word,
holding a voice that comes only through the pen,
silenced by the look, half a decade old,
reawakened by the western dawn.

The last face is no more, if it ever was,
now only the amorphous fog fit to form:
amorous, untouchable, unrequitable, unknowable,
atrophied through a lack of need,
fallen prey to life's life.

Inside the fog, there is nothing.
That alone will remain when the fog rolls,
the word breaks, the angel laughs, and the sand clears.
All the nothing left is incapable of causing a shadow.
The cave wall remains illuminated, undisturbed, undisturbable.

Artifice

There is a sort of peace now for the Nemean Lion,
    a certain desperation has left his looks.
"No more," cried Heracles, "will that foul beast
    prey on innocent blood fallen from the mouths of babes."
The lion does not protest this accusation
    he lies amicably on his side, tongue lolling from his gaping mouth,
    and in this game of life we each have our roles.

There is a sort of accidental nature to it all,
    that from Goliath's perspective David should be his killer.
Mordred's mind argues that Arthur is unjust
    railing against his father's order because it's all he knows.
We each fall into our own perspectives
    relying on our own artifice to preserve the natural world
    because we drink the dye to make reality cry fallacy.

We are the new Odysseus tied with broken knots
    to the splintering mast of our faltering bark.
The wax men ready their oars to shatter Poseidon's pain,
    and we climb the edge of the gang wall shedding our riggings.
In our efforts to reach the mystical virgin rocks
    we cling to them as they sink beneath the waves
    drawn together, blameless to our own ends.

Asclepius's punishment for fixing the salt king's son
    demonstrates the state we have always been in.
There is something to be said for a society punishing
    most those who have worked to improve the world.
We sit huddled in our darkened caves, chained and dripping with salve
    kept apart because we wanted to help
    not knowing that we always picked the wrong side.

Our stories give us the shades, the spirits that wander
    through the darkened edifices of our consciousness.
We quagmire ourselves beside the river Styx, content in Dis
    while those lording over us redefine our reality as they see fit.
Are there any left among us to feel sorry for Goliath or the lion,
    are the sirens more loathsome than Asclepius,
        are we any less guilty of their deaths as we watch the show unfold?

Antihero

When I stand and look out at the rain,
safely inside, warm and dry,
I don't think of the homeless and poor
as I probably should.
Instead I look at the crying skies
and think of my own children,
of the future they may have
and the world I will leave to them.
I think of melting glaciers, rising tides,
stronger storms, and changing climates
of war, destruction, death, and hate,
xenophobia, fear, pain, and anger—

Then they laugh

and that soft sound, like the uptick of spring winds,
roars though the house
drawing my attention from the window,
and I'm reminded to pray.

Our Father, Who aren't around us
Missing be Thy Name;
Thy kingdom done,
Thy will ignored,
on earth as we lose compassion
Give us this day some restitution,
and forgive us our callousness,
as we ignore *those who* need help and have less;
and lead us not into destruction,
but deliver us from ourselves.
For we are all selfish,

wandering, but hopeful *forever. Amen.*

I know I am not important on the grand scale,
I will never be able to save anyone,
but I watch my children play and hope
somehow they can learn from my failures.

A Good Day

Today is a good day
for water towers standing over treetops,
metal blooms to keep the torrents of water
off the ground.

Standing in parking lots
drowning in the water's shadow, watching
the bored rolling McDonald's bag languidly dancing
around the cracked pavement.

Sprouting from the cracks,
children, kept in place by their roots, wave at the sky.
They can only watch as clouds obscure the planes and the satellites
and drop a deluge on them.

When the clouds open,
carrying with them the nutrients of a polluted world,
the children wail at the trees longing for the safety
once found among them.

Irrelevant

Welcome to the future . . .

I have worked hard all night
to get this prepared for you.
I have slaved over my keyboard, stove, shovel, hammer,
toiling to complete this.

Irrelevant

I want to do this, to help you.
I have been listening
and I want to do things right, the right way, the first time.
I want to make a difference.

Irrelevant

I am trying to open your eyes.
Expand your horizons,
show you a future, a masterpiece, a home, a life
you didn't think was possible.

Irrelevant

There is a world out there
begging people to see it.
Ages, past and future, trying, striving, fighting, loving,
to speak to you through me.

Irrelevant

I have devoted my life
to this, to helping you.
I want to write this, cook this, dig this, build this,
I love doing this.

Irrelevant

I am doing this for you,
can't you see that?
I want you to get more, be more, have more, strive for
more out of life.

Irrelevant

I am . . .

You are My Paraphrase

You are my paraphrase of life,
    a new look at the passions that burned in my youth
    in the time before the waters of experience supplanted the
        Promethean gift.
You are the fathomless river of experience,
    as yet unmeasured in space or time
    unbound to a path in this labyrinthian world.
You are the vision of my past and the song of my future,
    forever singing the siren's serenade of my blown youth
    forging ahead of me, helplessly watching your mistakes.
You are the foundation of tomorrow in the execution,
    the sky in which my hopes can soar through
    mysteries of lost discoveries found new through your eyes.

My own turbulent storm of doubt projected in you
    though I have lost the will once discovered
        and doubt my ability to find solid purchase in your future.
I will fight through the doubt and confusion of my own ignorance
        to find you in your innocent beauty.

You are my paraphrase of life,
    radiant among the fathomless motes of time
    to be found in the exquisite star of new life.

About the Author

E.A. Johnson can often be found chasing after one of those diabolically bipedal entities we often refer to with the innocuous moniker of "Toddler" or waking in the wee hours of the morning to quiet the nightly cries of the littlest member of my family. Otherwise, he's directing a play, correcting papers, planning lessons, climbing trees, remodeling my home in the woods, reading in the groggy wastes of the middle of the night (since those aforementioned entities don't sleep), or drinking black dark roast (or something with a little more bite). Oh yeah, sometimes he even gets a little writing in there too. You can find some of his poetry in *The Chaffey Review* (Spring 2010), *The Battered Suitcase* (Winter 2010), and *Writing Tomorrow* (February 2012).

If you enjoyed this collection, you can find more of E.A. Johnson's work or join his mailing list at ericjohnsonwriter.com.

Previous Publications

"A Resting Place" & "Transcention" originally published in *The Chaffey Review* no. IV (Spring 2010).

"Tasting Iron" & "Metamorphosis" originally published in *The Battered Suitcase Vol 3 Issue 3* (Winter 2010).

"Cityscapes", "The Vagabond Sings to his Nightingale", "Natural Derivative", & "Westbound" originally published in *Writing Tomorrow* (February 2012).

About the Press

Unsolicited Press is a small press in Portland, Oregon. The small press is fueled by voracious editors, all of whom are volunteers. The press began in 2012 and continues to produce stellar poetry, fiction, and creative nonfiction.

Learn more at www.unsolicitedpress.com.

www.ingramcontent.com/pod-product-compliance
Lightning Source LLC
Chambersburg PA
CBHW030122100526
44591CB00009B/495